This Books Belongs To:

____

"this book is dedicated to the entire Buffalo community for being strong and brave to overcome one of the worst storms in history. This book is dedicated to all those who have lost their lives our
city will live on but will never forget you. This book is also dedicated to all emergency services for the sacrifices you made to keep us safe"

Tyler wakes up
after he heres his
mom call his name
"Tyler time to go

back to school"

Tyler rushes
to the window
after hearing
loud truck noise

Are you ready to go
back to school Tyler
mom said? Tyler says
yes mom I can't wait
I hope all my friends
are there today and
ms. Majors too

BUS
STOP
COFFEE SHOP

Tyler sees
snow everywhere
on his way to the
bus stop

Tyler and

his classmates

return to school

hello Ms. Majors

we missed you

Ms. Majors ask the
class would anyone
like to share their
time at home after
being stuck in
the house

GRAPHICS

there was so much

snow it covered

all the cars

INFOGRAPHICS

our

windows and

doors was

frozen

INFOGRAPHICS

it was so

cold outside

the news said

it was in the

negatives

we saw

the police on

snow mobiles

from the window

Buffalo storm December 2022

9 798986 064932